Irish Railway Memories

A Decade of Change – 1984-1994

in photographs by Paul Haywood

Text © Paul Haywood, 2018.
First published in the United Kingdom, 2018,
by Stenlake Publishing Ltd.
Telephone: 01290 551122
www.stenlake.co.uk

ISBN 9781840338195

**The publishers regret that they cannot supply
copies of any pictures featured in this book.**

Title page: **CIE/IR 001-class**. The steam-era turntable, water tower and remains of the recently-demolished 4-track running shed distract the eye from the refuelling Irish Rail 015 at Sligo sidings in 1990. My presence had disturbed the "gentleman of the road" who had set up camp alongside the water tower, but we parted ways with a friendly wave. This photograph seems to emphasise the width of their 1,600mm (5ft 3in) "Irish Broad Gauge" track. Ireland's first railway, from Dublin to Kingstown (now Dun Laoghaire), used the British standard gauge of 1,435mm (4ft 8.½in). However, Ulster Railway had opened a line from Belfast to Lisburn with a width of 1,880mm (6ft 2in) and the Dublin and Drogheda Railway was heading north with a narrower gauge of 1,575mm (5ft 2in). To prevent a break of gauge between Belfast and Dublin, and to standardise what could have been a very complex range of gauges, the Board of Trade decreed that Ireland should adopt the compromise gauge width of 1,500mm (5ft 3in) and those existing railways were re-gauged accordingly. To the best of my knowledge, the Irish broad gauge is only used in two other countries – Australia (Victoria) and part of Brazil (São Paulo).

Left: British Rail's Leyland/BREL railbus R3 was built in 1982 and bought by NIR in 1983 – designated RB003 "Railbus". Its design was clearly based on the Leyland National bus body of the period and was bought for use on the Coleraine to Portrush shuttle. It was not a success and was withdrawn in 1992 and presented to the Ulster Folk and Transport Museum. It again saw brief service on the Lisburn to Antrim branch in 2000 (then under threat of closure) but is now on display at the Downpatrick Railway Museum. It is seen between services at Coleraine in 1989.

Introduction

Although I have travelled extensively to ride and photograph trains and trams since 1970, I'm ashamed to admit that I didn't set foot onto the island of Ireland until 1984. Most of my early visits were for business so my photographs were based on station scenes taken before, during or after a rail journey. However, in the intervening years I now realise that I was lucky to have witnessed an era which is now long gone.

On my first visit, most of the Irish railway network had un-welded track, line-side telegraph poles and semaphore signalling. In the Republic, Córas Iompair Éireann (CIE), after an earlier dalliance with diesel railcars, was now almost totally a locomotive and carriage system requiring numerous labour intensive and time-consuming run-rounds at terminals. Much as I (and many others) loved their locomotives and coaches, their network simply cried out for railcars to simplify operations and make them more flexible. However, that was to come some years later.

Meanwhile, Northern Ireland Railways were almost totally the opposite, being heavily-dependent on ageing diesel-electric railcars for all but the cross-border services and occasional commuter runs.

As I hope to show in these pages, the period chosen for this book, 1984 to 1994, covers a decade when peaks of optimism would give way to troughs of pessimism almost annually, depending on the latest whim of the Dáil or Westminster politicians and civil servants. However, unlike many countries where the railways were deliberately run down, the island of Ireland now enjoys levels of rail service undreamed of, and Irish Rail (Iarnród Éireann) now has one of Europe's youngest fleets.

Irish railways have changed considerably since the decade of this book. Not only have Iarnród Éireann gone over to an almost nationwide railcar operation, NIR (now Translink) have revitalised their network with a fleet of new railcars on improved schedules (although there are still some improvements to be made).

I have gleaned much information from various publications to hopefully add interest to my captions, including *Irish Railways – 40 Years of Change* by Colin Boocock, and *35 Years of NIR* by Jonathan M. Allen, to whom I express thanks.

My photos are presented in the order of CIE then NIR rolling stock – by age, type and fleet number. Inevitably, there will be errors in my captions and I will have failed to refer to something important, but this is a snapshot of my rail travels between 1984 and 1994, not a definitive history of Irish railways.

If you are familiar with the railways of Ireland, I hope these photographs rekindle happy memories. For those unfamiliar with them, I hope this will encourage you to make a visit and ride their rails. You won't be disappointed – unless, of course, you *hate* modern railcars!

CIE/IR 001-class. The incredible 64-lever signal gantry at Waterford frames Irish Rail 020 in 1989. This signal box, built circa 1930, controlled the station and part of the adjacent freight yard, but was recently closed because of a nearby cliff rock-fall and changes to the signalling procedures in the area.

CIE/IR 001-class. CIE 022 is seen at Cork in 1984 with two CIE Inchicore-built "Laminate" coaches dating from the 1950s, on a Mallow/Tralee duty. Originally called Glanmire Road, now Kent, the present Cork station opened in 1893 replacing two separate stations – one for the Dublin line and one for the line to Youghal and Queenstown (Cobh). The only line going south at the time of this view was to Cobh, following the closure of the Youghal line to passengers in 1963 and freight in 1982. However, part of this line reopened for passenger traffic in 2009 as far as Midleton, running alternately with the Cobh service.

CIE/IR 001-class. Irish Rail 051 is at Dublin Connolly in 1994, waiting to get the right-of-way to proceed south to Shelton Abbey with its ammonia train, following the departure of the Bray-bound DART train. Formerly known as Amiens Street, this station has two distinct parts. The terminal platforms (under the former Great Northern shed roof in the background) serve Belfast and Sligo. The through platforms in the foreground continue south across the River Liffey to Dublin Pearse and the east coast line to Rosslare, following the opening of the City of Dublin Junction Railway in 1891. They were, in effect, two stations with separate entrances until the amalgamation of the southern portion of the GNR lines into the CIE empire in 1958. Since the start of DART services, this double-track cross-river line through Pearse has been a bottleneck, but recent resignalling has enabled a more intensive frequency on the section.

CIE/IR 001-class. Another lost freight movement is that of the Bell liner trains which ran from Waterford to Dublin North Wall and Belfast. 052 waits for clearance onto the single track at Thomastown, en route to Waterford container yard in 1990. The fine Tudor-Revival station building dates from 1848, when the Waterford and Kilkenny Railway reached here from Kilkenny, and is now an historic listed structure.

CIE/IR 001-class. A final look at these iconic locos. 055 was at Ballybrophy in 1992 waiting to receive passengers from a Dubin-Cork train onto this Limerick via Nenagh service. Soon after withdrawal in 1994, this locomotive was purchased by the owner of a bar and railway artefact museum called "Hell's Kitchen" in Castlerea, Co. Rosscommon. The loco is kept inside the premises and its engineless interior acts as a walkway between the bar and fascinating museum. 055 is now painted in an earlier CIE green, bearing its original number A55.

CIE 201-class. The CIE 201-class (formerly C-class) Metropolitan-Vickers Bo-Bo's dated from 1957 and were designed for light-duty branch line operation. Like their elder and bigger 001-class sisters, they were originally fitted with Crossley engines, but only rated at a measly 550hp. Unsurprisingly, these proved to be underpowered as well as unreliable and were similarly refitted with General Motors 1,100hp engines in the late 1970s, doubling their power overnight. 227 is seen at Dublin Connolly with a suburban service from Bray, soon to be replaced by the new DART (Dublin Area Rapid Transit) electric service – note the newly-erected overhead wires. The recently-applied "S" under the fleet number meant that it had been fitted with CAWS (Continuous Automatic Warning System) then being introduced. After a period of work with NIR (as their 106), this loco was saved for preservation but is now reported to be in a very poor condition. However, two others of this class are preserved in good order (226 and 231).

CIE/IR 121-class. After the problems experienced with the unreliable Crossley engines in the late 1950s, CIE were desperate to find a reliable source of new locomotives. To the surprise of many, they approached General Motors (US) and bought fifteen of these single-ended Bo-Bo locos in 1960, based on the EMD GL8 "road-switchers". This was GM's first export of complete locomotives into Europe and they were fitted with a 960hp engine which proved to be both reliable and economical. However, because CIE drivers weren't used to driving from a trailing cab, they were soon only allowed to be run cab-first which limited their use and meant that many steam-era turntables had to be kept in service. In later years, some were semi-permanently coupled back-to-back like 129+122 at Dublin Heuston in 1984.

CIE/IR 121-class. Some of the last regular duties for the 121-class were on the Outer Suburban push-pull trains from Dublin Pearse to Drogheda and Dundalk. However, because these 6-coach sets were too heavy for their 960hp motors, they were fitted with 1,100hp motors taken from redundant 201-class locos. These push-pull sets were comprised of a 121-class running cab-first with five coaches and a driving trailer (see page 28). All these specially-modified Inchicore-built Mark 3 coaches had their air cooling equipment removed and replaced with forced-air ventilation hopper windows. 130 is seen at Connolly about to depart with a short 3-coach + driving trailer non-revenue test train in 1990. As an aside, I doubt if anyone at GM could ever have imagined that what were effectively "freight yard switchers" would be used on heavy-duty commuter services like these, some 30 years after being built.

CIE/IR 141-class. Following on from the success of the 121-class, CIE had no hesitation in going back to GM for their next batch of locos. This time they wanted double-ended equipment and in 1962 bought 37 of these 141-class Bo-Bo's with 960hp engines, which were known as "dog bones" because of their full width cabs and narrow bodies. Once again they proved to be versatile and reliable, soon becoming the CIE's workhorses for most non-express operations. Here is 144 passing through Lisburn (NI) in 1990 on another lost freight duty – a Bell liner train to Adelaide yard, Belfast.

CIE/IR 141-class. The driver of 146 slows to exchange tokens with the signalman at Clonmel in 1989. This train from Waterford to Limerick was made up of three Park Royal coaches and a former British Rail coach which was converted to a generator van by CIE. At that time, most passenger trains needed to have a steam or electric heat and power generator van attached at one end of each rake of carriages. For me, this was yet another reason why a change to diesel railcars had to be the most sensible option, much as we might now miss the charm of this traditional operation.

CIE/IR 141-class. A reminder of the once-common sight of steam escaping from carriages and the ubiquitous generator van at Cobh in 1994. 165 is about to pull forward into the head shunt before running round its train of BR generator van and three Craven coaches. Cobh (pronounced cove) was once the major Irish seaport for transatlantic passengers and mail (formerly known as Queenstown). One of its most infamous claims to fame was as the final port-of-call for the *Titanic*, although the ship had to moor off-shore as the harbour couldn't handle that size of vessel. Today, cruise liners dock alongside this now modernised station. This attractive branch line was one of the first to be handed over to the new era of Japanese-built railcars from the mid-1990s so the need to operate this point switch would soon disappear.

CIE/IR 141-class. CIE 169 is seen at Dublin Connolly with a rake of NIR "Enterprise" stock in 1984. Unfortunately, I can't remember whether it was about to perform an "Enterprise" duty or was just removing the empty stock from the platform for servicing. Note the fencing on the platform. This was, for many years, a feature of the Belfast platform at Connolly, dating from a period when (often cursory) customs and security checks were made on the platform.

CIE/IR 141-class. Five years later, we see 169 again, this time wearing its Irish Rail logo in the head shunt of Kilkenny's freight yard in 1989. Unsurprisingly, this freight yard is now a car park and the head shunt mound has been flattened to create a widened road down at street level. As an aside, the traffic lights seen in the background remind me of a taxi journey I took from this station. At these lights, a car in front of us failed to pull away immediately when they went to green. My taxi driver, having been delayed for a few precious seconds, exclaimed "For crying out loud, they're not going to get any greener!"

CIE/IR 141-class. The attractive terminal station at Killarney dates from 1853 when the line from Mallow opened. When the line was extended to Tralee in 1859, it took an avoiding alignment but with access to the station from a facing junction. This required trains to Tralee to enter forward and reverse out, and for Mallow-bound trains to reverse in and drive out. 170 and its Craven coaches had just arrived from Tralee having reversed into the station before continuing forward to Mallow and Cork in 1994.

CIE/IR 181-class. CIE were very pleased with the performance of their 141-class and in 1966 ordered a further twelve almost identical locos from GM which were fitted with a larger (1,100hp) engine and designated 181-class. 183 stands in the Cobh platform at Cork in 1989. The suffixes S and A signified it had been fitted with a Continuous Automatic Warning System (CAWS) and air brakes – both being introduced from the early 1980s – but these suffixes were dropped once all the fleet had been dealt with. Note the Travelling Post Office coaches which were still being used on a nightly mail sorting run to and from Dublin until this operation ceased in 1994.

CIE/IR 071-class. By the mid-1970s the 001-class were starting to show their age and there was a need for more powerful Co-Co locomotives for express duties. Once again, CIE went back to GM (now the EMD plant in Canada) for this batch of eighteen larger and more powerful locos (2,450hp) capable of 90mph running. In 1984 we see CIE 074 at Belfast Central (due to be renamed Belfast Lanyon Place in September 2018) with its usual rake of BREL-built Mark 2d coaches. This was the very first CIE train I saw, photographed and rode on. Being very familiar with the coaches (externally at least) it seemed strange to see and hear this unusual beast at the front with its distinctive GM tick-over chime. The journey was, I remember, uneventful except for watching what seemed like scores of army helicopters filling the skies around Newry, and the memory of a simple evening meal in the restaurant/buffet car which automatically came with a pot of tea and a plate of bread and butter, bringing a sense of calm to my first experience of a troubled world. Later in the journey I had the obligatory can of Guinness which at the time seemed a nice traditional pastime. However, I soon became frustrated by the lack of beer and lager choices on offer anywhere in Ireland, being the same old triumvirate of stout (usually Guinness, sometimes Murphys or occasionally my preferred Beamish), fizzy Harp lager and Smithwick ale. Thankfully, in later years, locally-produced real ale and craft beers have allowed more choice … but that's another story.

CIE/IR 071-class. The 071-class locomotives were needed for the revamped express duties from Dublin to Cork. These, together with new BR-designed, CIE-built Mark 3 coaches introduced from the mid-1980s, gave CIE a real marketing coup for inter-city travel in Ireland. Now sporting its new Irish Rail logo and livery, 085 awaits departure from Cork to Dublin Heuston in 1988. For those unfamiliar with this location, the train will exit the station and immediately run into a steeply-graded 1,240 metre long tunnel opened in 1855.

CIE/IR 071-class. In the 1960s, CIE changed from what was considered to be an appropriate "Irish" livery of green, to what can only be described as "black and tan" which still has political resonance for many. 087 stands in the Cork platform of Dublin Heuston Station in 1984, coupled to a new Mark 3 generator and guards van. This station (formerly known as Kingsbridge) opened in 1846 and is Ireland's most important station with lines radiating to most parts of the country except the Rosslare, Belfast and Sligo routes served by Connolly. Like many large cities with early railways, terminal stations were often located outside the central areas and transferring between here and Connolly was always a problem. Now, thanks to a new tramway link, this journey is far easier and more comfortable than the traffic-snarled rail-link buses used to be.

CIE/IR 071-class. 087 again, this time in the later IR livery of orange and black with white, as it enters Ballybrophy with a train from Heuston in 1992. To the left is the Limerick via Nenagh train which has been waiting for this connection to arrive. It consists of two Park Royal coaches and a Dutch (Werkspoor/Dundalk) generator van, with Metro-Vic 001-class 055 at the head. The 90km line from here to Limerick via Nenagh had, and still has, a very infrequent service which, although being geographically shorter than taking the main line via Limerick Junction, takes almost an hour longer. Consequently, there has been recurring talk of closure thanks to a spiral of poor service equalling low use.

IE 201-class. A new dawn breaks. In the early 1990s, in the face of an almost worldwide trend towards fixed-formation diesel and electric railcars and units, Iarnród Éireann decided to stay with loco haulage. Paramount in this decision was the expectation of a boom in freight traffic requiring extra tractive effort. Thirty-two of these 3,200hp Co-Co 201 "River"-class locos were delivered from GM (Canada) in 1994-95 which soon found their way onto the fastest duties and heaviest freights. One of the last photos I took during the decade covered by this book is of almost-new 203 "River Corrib", complete with the new IE (Iarnród Éireann) logo and colour scheme, at Dublin Heuston in September 1994. Their reign proved to be short-lived however, and within the next decade many Irish passenger duties would go over to diesel railcar operation. Furthermore, sadly, much of the anticipated freight traffic would not materialise. This led to the premature withdrawal and storage of these fine machines. Now, their use is restricted to the push-pull Cork and "Enterprise" services plus occasional freight and charter trains. Against the advice of GM, they were all fitted with Head End Power to supply heat and power for "Enterprise" duties which use specially-built sets of coaches with no generator van in the formation. This would add to IE's problems, as the 201-class locos used on the "Enterprise" failed at an alarming rate due to the stresses caused by the constant high revs needed to maintain on-board power, even when stationary. In recent years, redundant Mark 3 generator vans have been added to the "Enterprise" sets to avoid this problem.

CIE/IR coaching stock. A BR generator/guards van and three Park Royal/CIE coaches dating from 1955 reverse into the "Waterford bay" at the isolated interchange station of Limerick Junction in 1989. The station is on the Dublin/Cork line which runs in an approximate north/south direction. However, the route of this train from Limerick to Waterford runs in an approximate west to east direction, crossing the Cork main line at right-angles just to the north of the station. It is hard to describe the complex manoeuvres required to get this train into and out of this station, but suffice it to say it involved much reversing (with passengers on board). This included the use of this "back line", the opening and closing of the level crossing gates and running into the distant head shunt, just to get the train into and out of this south-facing platform. The more recent introduction of railcars on connecting services has led to a simplification of the station layout and these tracks have been lifted to create a park-and-ride facility.

CIE/IR coaching stock. These unusual steam generator/guards vans were built in 1969 by Werkspoor (Netherlands) in collaboration with Dundalk Engineering. It is seen at Kilkenny in March, 1994 during its enforced layover to allow 071-class 088 to run round its train whilst parcels are removed from the van. Kilkenny was once a through station with a line continuing to Portlaoise which closed in 1963. Because of the loss of this direct route off the Dublin line at Portlaoise, trains now had to perform an out-and-back manoeuvre from a "y" junction off the Waterford via Carlow line a few miles to the east. This meant that locomotives had to run round their trains at this head shunt under the station canopy (as seen). Since 2011, following the introduction of railcars, the tracks now finish at approximately the position of this van, and the head shunt tracks have been removed, allowing a paved walkway for passengers to reach the adjacent platform, previously only accessible by a footbridge.

CIE/IR coaching stock. On my first trip to Ireland in 1984 I was thrilled to see these examples of new BREL-designed, CIE-built Mark 3 coaches at Dublin Heuston waiting to perform a Cork service. They had electric plug doors which offered improved safety over the traditional British slam door arrangement. However, they suffered initial teething problems with the mechanism and I remember lengthy announcements having to be made at each stop to ensure their safe use when boarding and alighting. Today, the concept of having self-opening slam doors on scheduled express trains is unthinkable, thanks to innovations like this back in 1984.

CIE/IR coaching stock. CIE were enthusiastic users of their Mark 3 coaches which, by necessity, needed these electric generator/guards vans to supply heat and power to the formation. This example is seen at Limerick Junction en route to Dublin in 1989, with a connecting service for Limerick at the adjacent platform. Important as this station is, the nearest community (Tipperary) is some 5 km away. It is, and always has been, an isolated point of interchange between north/south and east/west trains. Today, however, the station has been extensively rebuilt and is now a major park-and-ride facility for the region.

IR coaching stock. The final batch of Mark 3 coaches that were being built at Inchicore Works was amended to create these push-pull sets for use on Outer Suburban services from Dublin Pearse to Drogheda and Dundalk (see page 11). Driving/generator trailer 6102 is at the end of a short, non-revenue, test train about to head north from Connolly in 1990. When railcars took over these services, these push-pull formations were used on other routes, making operations more flexible prior to the wholesale introduction of railcars system wide.

CIE/IR DART. No book on Irish railways is complete without mention of the excellent Dublin Area Rapid Transit (DART) operation then running from Howth to Bray via Connolly. These electric units, built by Linke-Hoffman-Busch/GEC in 1983/4, opened the service just months after this view of brand-new driving trailer 8326 was taken at Dublin Pearse (formerly Westland Row) in 1984. It was on display for commuters to see what a tremendous improvement they would experience against the cramped and spartan Park Royal or similar carriages then used on coastal suburban services. I apologise for my obvious trespass to get this photo, but the station was almost devoid of passengers and staff and train frequences were then very low. How different things are today, as Pearse is the second busiest station in Ireland, thanks to DART. It is also claimed to be the world's first "commuter" station, having been the city terminus of the Dublin to Kingstown (now Dun Laoghaire) Railway which opened in 1834.

CIE/IR DART. A 2 x2-car set of LHB electrics, led by driving trailer 8305, rolls into Landsdowne Road Station in 1989, under the now-demolished west stand of the famous national rugby ground. Since then, DART services have been extended south from Bray to Greystones along the cliff-hugging alignment surveyed by Brunel, and north from Howth Junction to Malahide. DART has revolutionised Dublin commuter operations and plans for expansion are ongoing.

NIR 101-class. We now turn our attention to Northern Ireland Railways and this unusual Hunslet/BREL/English Electric Bo-Bo loco dating from 1970. 101 "Eagle" was one of three bought for "Enterprise" push-pull duties and their 1,350hp engines ensured they were able to match the CIE 001-class timings on the joint service. When introduced, they were the only locos in Ulster in what was then a totally diesel railcar province. Following the introduction of NIR's GM 111-class in 1981, they were relegated to occasional passenger, freight, permanent way and shunting operations like this fertiliser train duty in Londonderry in 1990. Following withdrawal this loco was stored at the Railway Preservation Society of Ireland's Whitehead railway museum, but was cannibalised for spares for preserved sister 102 and scrapped in 2010. Note the distinctive clock-tower of the former Waterside Railway Station, built in 1873 by the Belfast and Northern Counties Railway. Part of it was bombed in 1975 which led to the station being moved to this new position in 1980.

NIR 111-class. The superior performance of the CIE 071-class on "Enterprise" duties did not go unnoticed by NIR. By the late 1970s their 101-class locomotives were starting to show their age so NIR bought two locos identical to the 071-class from GM in 1981. The first, 111 "Great Northern", is seen at Belfast Central in 1988. In those days, waiting for a train at Central Station was not a pleasant experience and the high security fence is a reminder of those troubled times.

NIR 111-class. The second loco of the pair was 112 "Northern Counties" having just arrived into Belfast Central from Dublin with a mix of BREL-built Mark 2b and 2c coaches and generator van in 1988. Note my "Please do not leave baggage unattended" error. Having just got off this train I ran over the footbridge with suitcase and briefcase to take this shot. No doubt the driver was pleased to know that they were mine when I retrieved them.

NIR 111-class. It soon became clear that two of this class was not sufficient to fulfil requirements, so a third was ordered from GM (EMD) for delivery in 1984. 113 "Belfast and County Down" is seen entering Dublin Connolly with rake of "Enterprise" stock in July 1984. This photo was a Kodachrome slide and the mount is imprinted "Jul 84". At the time, I didn't give the date much attention, but in later years it seemed to be at odds with all the written evidence which gave 113's entry into service as August 1984. It is now thought to have been seen on its very first passenger duty on a pre-handover proving run. Sadly, I have lost my diary for 1984 so cannot give a specific date other than "mid to late July".

NIR 104-class. Six of these CIE 201-class locos dating from 1957 were bought by NIR between 1985 and 1987 in the expectation of new freight traffic from a proposed movement of fuel to a power station and of municipal waste to a disposal site, neither of which materialised. Consequently they were used mainly on permanent way, shunting and light freight duties. Here is NIR 104 (formerly CIE 216) with a ballast train at Lisburn in 1988. It was last used in 1994 and scrapped in 1997.

NIR 70-class railcar. The 70-class railcars were built in 1966 by the Ulster Transport Authority, and fitted with an English Electric 550hp motor in the front car. 72 "River Foyle" wore this Sealink livery from 1983 until 1985 and is seen at Belfast Central in 1984. It promoted the Belfast-Larne/Stranraer-Glasgow rail/ferry/rail service, and was matched by a BR unit with the same livery in Scotland. However, the Belfast York Road to Larne line was then effectively isolated from the main network until the opening of the cross-harbour rail link in 1994, so this unit only saw limited service on its promoted route. It was withdrawn in 1985 and scrapped in 1986. Following withdrawal in the mid-1980s, the motors from these sets were refurbished for use in the new 450-class (see page 46).

NIR 80-class railcar. These 3-car diesel-electric railcars were affectionately nicknamed "Thumpers" because of the noise their English Electric motors made. They were built by BREL Derby between 1974 and 1978 using Mark 2b body shells and fitted with an English Electric 560hp motor and became the prime movers in Northern Ireland. The contrasting ends of these units is evident in this view of driving trailer 744 and driving motor 91 as they stand in Bangor Station in 1988.

NIR 80-class railcar. Between 1987 and 1990, Irish Rail leased three of these units to cover a shortage of rolling stock and applied their IR logo to each car. Driving motor 68 stands at Bray awaiting a turn on the Greystones shuttle in 1988. Sadly, because of its infrequent schedule, I was unable to ride it over this scenic cliff-hugging route.

NIR 80-class railcar. Standing at Cork in 1988 is IR-logo driving motor 69 on the Cobh service. In December, 2013 this whole platform canopy, dating from 1893, was blown onto its side during a severe gale, injuring one person and damaging a railcar. It was repaired at an estimated cost of €3m. 69 was subsequently preserved and is now at the Downpatrick and County Down Railway wearing its first livery of maroon and blue.

NIR 80-class railcar. The third IR service using the leased NIR 80-class was Dublin Connolly to Maynooth. Driving motor 69 had now moved from Cork to Dublin and is seen at Connolly in September 1990 nearing the end of its lease period.

NIR 80-class railcar. For a few months after their return to NIR the leased sets continued to wear the IR logo. Driving trailer 740 had just arrived at Portadown with a cross-city train from Bangor in September 1990. Note the new Suburban-sector livery at the driving motor end.

NIR 80-class railcar. In 1987 NIR decided to split its organisation into "sectors", being InterCity, Suburban and Freight. Inevitably, this required new liveries, like that worn by this Suburban-sector set, with driving motor 81 "The Boys Brigade" pushing its train north out of Lisburn in 1990. Like many modern UK bus and train companies, NIR then believed that a change of livery and corporate colour scheme would encourage greater patronage and improve the public image. Of course, what really mattered was the quality of service not the image. During their long life, these units have worn at least six different colour schemes, but I believe this one was perhaps the most interesting.

NIR 80 class railcar. York Road was one of three original Belfast terminals, each belonging to a different railway company. York Road was, after Grouping, operated by the LMS-owned Northern Counties Committee Railway running to Londonderry and Larne. Following the circuitous re-routing of the Londonderry line from the newly-opened Central Station via Lisburn, York Road's role diminished and this once fine station was reduced to little more than a brick waiting room and platforms for the now-isolated Larne line. This station finally closed in 1992 in preparation for the long-awaited cross-harbour link to Central which in turn saw the eventual revival of the more direct Londonderry service. Here we see driving motor 97 "Glenshesk" having a wash-and-brush-up before its Larne duty in 1985.

NIR 80-class railcar. Driving trailer 735 arrives into Ballymoney in 1994, en route to Londonderry. This Belfast to Londonderry train then used the circuitous route from Central via Lisburn and Knockmore Junction to reach Antrim, following the closure of the more direct route from York Road and Bleach Green. The subsequent opening of the cross-harbour link and the reopening of the Bleach Green route once again gave passengers a more convenient and useful service. Sadly, the line from Lisburn and Knockmore Junction to Antrim closed to regular traffic soon after, although there have been numerous plans for it to re-open. The impressive station canopies look to be made of timber but were in fact made of cast iron, dating from when this station was rebuilt to a "cottage style" in 1902.

NIR 80-class railcar. Bomb scares were, and unfortunately still are, a regular occurrence on Northern Ireland's railways – thankfully most are hoaxes but sometimes they are for real. Both railway companies take these threats seriously, causing massive disruption to passengers and staff. The railways, however, have always done their best to keep services running in difficult circumstances. This is one example, when the threat of a bomb on the line south of Newry prevented IR's northbound "Enterprise" from proceeding north from Dundalk in 1992. To fulfil its southbound duty, NIR laid on this 2 x 3-car train (appropriately wearing the latest InterCity livery), led by 99 "Sir Myles Humphries". It had worked from Belfast as far as here at Newry, where passengers were transferred onto buses for the run over the border to Dundalk to board the waiting and much-delayed IR train to Dublin.

NIR 450-class railcar. When the 70-class railcars were coming to the end of their lives, NIR needed replacements but money was tight. An economical solution was found by using refurbished 70-class English Electric motors and traction equipment, using former BR Mark 1 underframes and new bodies built by BREL Derby based on the BR 210-class design. The first three of these 450-class were delivered in 1985 and, because the exercise was successful, a further six were delivered the following year. Needless to say, these new railcars needed a new livery (as seen). My first reaction to these railcars was mixed. It was pleasing to see power-operated doors and a clean, modern interior, but it came as a surprise to hear the roar of the twenty-year old English Electric "Thumper" motors which somehow didn't match their new image. Driving trailer 784 leads the set at Belfast York Road in 1990.

NIR 450-class railcar. In 1987, following the "sectorisation" of NIR into Suburban, InterCity and Freight divisions, more new liveries started to appear. All the 450-class were allocated to the Suburban sector but not all received its livery. However, 452 *Olderfleet Castle* was, I am led to believe, seen in the throes of having a Suburban-sector livery applied as it passed through the paint shop of Belfast York Road depot in 1990.

NIR 450-class railcar. Driving trailer 786 stands at the buffers at Larne Harbour Station in 1994. It is now wearing the corporate InterCity livery which was applied to all rolling stock (but minus the word InterCity on some railcars) following the abandonment of the sectors in 1991. This was an important transfer point for foot passengers travelling by rail and sea to Glasgow via the Sealink ferry to Stranraer. Sadly, this historic rail/sea/rail journey has now been severed thanks to P&O's decision to cease using Stranraer in favour of Cairnryan which has no rail link.

NIR 450-class railcar. Our final look at this class of railcar sees driving motor 458 "Antrim Castle" at the temporary terminus of Belfast Yorkgate in 1994 which replaced York Road Station in 1992. Beyond is the cross-harbour rail link which would eventually connect the isolated Larne line with Central Station and, from 1995, the reopened Great Victoria Street station. This long-awaited elevated bridge link had first been mooted as far back as 1977 and after a series of on/off hiatuses was eventually opened for traffic at the end of 1994. However, because of budget constraints, what was hoped would be a double-track bridge was built as single-track with passing loop which severely limits its potential.